The Lowercase Jew

RODGER KAMENETZ

The Lowercase Jew

TRIQUARTERLY BOOKS
NORTHWESTERN UNIVERSITY PRESS
EVANSTON, ILLINOIS

TriQuarterly Books
Northwestern University Press
Evanston, Illinois 60208-4210

Printed in the United States of America

10 9 8 7 6 5 4 3 2 1

ISBN 0-8101-5151-0 (cloth)
ISBN 0-8101-5152-9 (paper)

Library of Congress Cataloging-in-Publication Data

Kamenetz, Rodger, 1950–
   The lowercase Jew / Rodger Kamenetz.
    p. cm.
   ISBN 0-8101-5151-0 (cloth : alk. paper) — ISBN 0-8101-5152-9 (pbk. : alk. paper)
   1. Jews—Poetry. 2. Judaism—Poetry. I. Title.
  PS3561.A4172 L68 2003
  811'.54—dc21

                                                    2003009957

Letterpress cover printed by Jennifer Thomas

In memory, Amy Scherr Stoltz and Blanche Markowitz.
You dear sweet people in heaven.

CONTENTS

The Lowercase Jew

PART ONE

Grandfather Clause

Grandfather Clause

For David Kamenetz, *z"l*

If only you'd done what you'd been told to do.
If only you'd not been lifted by a chance wind
west above the wheat tips of the Ukraine,
the thunder of knouts, the Cossacks shouting.
If you had stayed instead to be murdered,
the *Einzatsgruppen,* old men like you,
fingers palsied on the trigger, bellies shaking at the recoil,
would have shot you dead at the edge of a pit,
slaughtered you on the outskirts of a town
Jews could not enter after sundown.

There is a clause that refers to you
in the inner lining of a foreign language
where *Jew* is the dirtiest word ever.
This clause prepared in advance of your name
is the secret history of your death
decreed in a grammar strange to your Yiddish
as the language I speak is still inflected
by the death that might have been.

Yet you entered America like a pilgrim or a germ.
Which was it? Or both, as America decided,
with your Jewish heart and lungs, and your Jewish disease,
and two strong fingers and a needle.

Why should I tell that old story again?
I'm still immigrating into this moment, learning
that the words applied to you apply to me.
Even after all this time, I will not allow anyone
to annihilate your name and mine.
I am grandfathered in.

Poem-in-Law

My third cousin, twice removed, owes me a thousand.
He lives in the caves of doubt, he phones me late
in code. "Mountains of wind," he cries and click.
"Grains of doubt." Leaves me to decode,
cold, looking for my damn slippers. Rocks
in the mail, carefully packaged, stamps from
Mysore and lines from Irving Layton.
"Poems-in-law!" hisses through the receiver,
travels in a forest of voices
on its way to my ear. I hang up, I interpret.
My cousin has paid me back a thousand times.
Irving, I say, get a job. Send me five
a week, there are enough days. He bows
seven times and bites my neck. "Do I owe
you? That's 'Am I my brother's keeper?'
multiplied into debt, doubt. Do I owe you
when the wind is free and rocks cost
nothing? I've paid you back
within an inch of my life and you talk about
money? If you were really a poet you'd be
skimming gold from molten lead, your hair
singed, your eyebrows on fire.
You'd lick the bottom of the vat, you'd swim
in honey. You wouldn't worry about money orders.
Angels would call you collect. And the grand muse
with mechanical wings would creak overhead

blasting poems into your hair. Instead
all you've got is me, Irving, your poem-in-law.
Think I'm going to stop?
Try to stop breathing. It's easier."

A Dead Jew's Eyes

On the eightieth anniversary of the publication
of "The Waste Land." The speaker is Tom Eliot.

Toiling in the bank, wife half mad.
Father cutting off my funds.
I plunge in muck, unfathomable, blind.
Lobsters hourly keep close watch
Hark! now I hear them   scratch   scratch   scratch
scratching the floor of the mind.

Social insecurity, editorial distraction.
Scraping irritation, itching, the burning.
The Jews I had to scratch:
Otto Kahn offered cash.
Alfred Knopf said yes—in time
to placate Father, then I sank
Bleistein below the waterline.

Burning burning burning burning
O Lord Thou pluckest
burning
To quench a fire,
drown a Jew.

Full fathom five your Bleistein lies
Under the flatfish and the squids.
Graves' Disease in a dead jew's eyes!

When the crabs have eat the lids.
Though he suffer a sea-change
Still expensive rich and strange . . .

That was the finale I
sent to midwife Pound.
Not *Shantih shantih shantih,*
but *See upon his back he lies*
(Bones peep through the ragged toes)
With a stare of dull surprise

This is the way "The Waste Land" ends
This is the way "The Waste Land" ends
This is the way "The Waste Land" ends
not with a bang but a dead Jew's eyes,
a cartoon from *Der Stürmer.*

But Pound, ever helpful,
wrote question marks and *doubtful*
next to Bleistein's "Dirge."
I scratched the secret climax
that Phlebas the Phoenician,
drowned sailor of the tarot deck,
is baggy-pants Bleistein.

Lucky for me. For *various critics*
have done me the honour
to interpret the poem
as important . . . social criticism.
Lucky critics, spared glossing
a bloated Jew gnawed by crabs.
They could save their excuses for Pound,
for Heidegger and De Man.

The Lowercase Jew

T. S. Eliot stands before a heavenly court. A burlesque.

THE PROSECUTOR:

T.S., I got to tell you the *emes*—
Bleistein here, pardon the cigar.
Remember me, *palms turned out,*
Chicago Semite Viennese?
Like I'm some kind of ape?
You didn't like my baggy pants.
Now I'm here to take your measure.

To prosecute is dreck, but I got assigned.
You think God don't have a sense of humor?
It's punishment for you, but also me.
I have to read these *farkakta* lines
you wrote about the Jews.

Exhibit A:

The jew squats on the window sill, the owner,
Spawned in some estaminet in Antwerp—

Squats, what's the matter?
Did you owe your landlord rent?
And *spawned*—like shrimp in a tank?
Or in some dank cabaret after hours

two Jew toads humping on a table?
And what about that lowercase *j*?
You must have hated us
to break the rules of grammar,
most bank clerkly of Englishmen.

Still I got to admire your style,
the classy way you built those lines.
The sounds kick back and forth:
jew and *spawned, owner* and *Antwerp, squats*!
You've got a delicate ear.
The *w* sounds kiss word to word
before they stick in the craw.
But the lowercase *jew*
that spawned them all,
that I don't forgive.
You were a poet, T.S.,
you shoulda known better,
a guardian of the tongue.
That lowercase *j* was
a country-club sign.
NO DOGS OR JEWS ALLOWED.
To keep us out of the poem
or make us stoop to enter.

Exhibit B:

Rachel née Rabinovitch
Tears at the grapes with murderous paws;

Me, I'm an ape, okay.
Look what you did to poor Rachel.

A raccoon you made her.
That gorgeous girl with the dark eyes,
dead now fifty years.

I remember you liked to watch
her and the one in the Spanish cape.
You peeked in through the barroom door
in your bank-clerk suit buttoned up tight,
clutching your umbrella handle.

Premature dirty old man,
did you dream Rabinovitch,
a rabbi's daughter,
would softly claw your grapes?

If only you weren't so scared.
If only you had known her.
What a world of wonder she hid.
You were drawn by what was under,
and you were afraid too.
Undersea, under skirts,
the secret under-name
for the secret underneath
where you thought you might drown.

I should have been a pair of ragged claws
Scuttling across the floors of silent seas.

Pardon the dime-store Freud
from a Chicago Viennese,
but about yourself you didn't feel so good
so you took it out on me

and Rachel and Sir Ferdinand Klein.
Was he the only phony,
you fake English from Saint Louie, Missouri?

Were you ashamed
that you liked to sniff around
dirty bars, back alleys, looking
for rolled-up condoms on the ground?

testimony of summer nights

Hey, everyone's got a hobby.
Sweet and dirty, high and low,
Shakespeare and Dante in your ear,
slime in your eye, a stink in your nose.
You liked to mix it up.

London and Jerusalem,
you called them *unreal cities.*
Maybe what made those cities unreal
was you never saw the people in them.
Just toads, raccoons, apes—and rats.

For rats you had a special feel.

A rat crept softly through the vegetation
Dragging its slimy belly on the bank

rats feet over broken glass

And here's Exhibit C.

On the Rialto once.
The rats are underneath the piles.
The jew is underneath the lot.

That time in Venice
a Jew got between you and a painting
what did you see when you looked in his face?

A lustreless protrusive eye
Stares from the protozoic slime
At a perspective of Canaletto.

Protrusive eye? Protozoic slime? Canaletto?
You should plant your head like a potato
and grow your eyes underground!

Instead of rats,
you could have had *rakhmones,*
the love a mother feels in her belly.
You could have felt for people
like what you felt for rats.

I rest my case.

DEFENSE:

Sir Ferdinand Klein for the defense.
What Bleistein's done is most unfair.
Excerpts, scraps, bits and pieces.
Not the whole art, not the song.

Let's admit there's much that's ugly
in the fragments he's presented.

The world is also quite imperfect.
Do we then condemn creators?

These are only words in a poem,
and "poetry makes nothing happen."
A few bad moments for a Jew
in English class. Black people
and women have to take far worse.
If we must comb the crumbs of hate
from every line of verse,
there would be little left to read.

Without aversion, there is no passion.
Without abomination, no law.
Surely that's clear to a Jew.

JUDGE (*to Eliot*):

I wonder, do you think that so?
Does music have no power?
When Hitler wrote crude poems
on the walls of the heart,
like you he made a metaphor.
Jews were pests
and Zyklon-B, a pesticide.
To bad men, bad poetry
gives marching orders.

ELIOT:

But what, as Bleistein said, *rakh—, rakh—*
Christian mercy, he meant.

Surely you can't blame me
for what the Nazis did?
I wrote those lines before the war.
It was a different time.
My copyright expires soon,
punishment enough.
I'll be in public domain.

JUDGE:

All the worse. You never once apologized,
retracted, or removed those lines.
You published them up to the end.

ELIOT:

But I won a Nobel Prize. Surely—

JUDGE:

There are plenty of them in hell.

Come, stand before the golden scale
holding your book. "Gerontion,"
"Sweeney among the Nightingales,"
and "Bleistein with Cigar."
Here in the light, one particle of hate
weighs more than a lifetime of verse.

Your defense is your indictment.
Your judgment, your readership.
You will be read most fervently

by those who cannot read themselves.
Phonies, snobs, deluded social climbers,
pseudo-English fake professors
in bow ties and tweed, anachronisms,
wine snobs, false souls who preach
but cannot feel the pain of others,
hypocrite readers, your sisters, your brothers.

Now in the name . . .

BLEISTEIN:

Excuse me, Your Honor, we Jews have a sign
when we want to speak. We interrupt.

JUDGE:

What is your objection?

BLEISTEIN:

Condemned to his readers? That's too soft by half.
What punishment is that? They'll love him to death.
They'll excuse him in public, and in private they'll laugh.

JUDGE:

What more do you suggest?

BLEISTEIN:

If it please the court, purgatory.

JUDGE:

That's fine, but it's Catholic for Catholics
and Jewish for Jews. He's neither.

BLEISTEIN:

Send him from here
to Hyam Plutzik's grandson's bar mitzvah.
For the Jews it will seem an afternoon.
For him, a hundred years.

He'll hora with Rachel née Rabinovitch
and *kazatzki* with Allen Ginsberg
who will give him wet sloppy kisses
(it's okay, he's a little meshuga)
while his landlord, from that Antwerp nightclub,
leads the klezmer orchestra.

Put him at table 16 with Myron Cohen.
He'll torture him with jokes.
A million setups in English,
a million punch lines in Yiddish.
Then when he's hungry—for his delicate palate,
matzo ball soup with schmaltz on top, gallon after gallon,
and a thousand miles of dishes shaking glaucous jelly,
each with a *shtikl* gefilte fish stamped with a capital *J*.

ELIOT (*groaning*):

I am bound upon a bagel of fire.

JUDGE:

Silence. As the accused seems unrepentant,
we'll take Bleistein's suggestion to heart.

(*Turning to Eliot*)

And now in the name of the letter *J*
which every eye can see,
J that stands for *Jehovah,*
Jesus, but also for *Jew*—
that little *j* you left behind
now stands for *justice* too.

BLEISTEIN (*aside*):

Poets, you should be careful the words you choose.
Remember, there are no lowercase Jews.

Allen Ginsberg Forgives Ezra Pound
on Behalf of the Jews

This is something I was too shy to ask you in that interview.
Was it arrogance, your public relations brilliance,
some deep desire to heal the split in American poesy,
a rascally *fuck you* to all the rabbis you never loved,
the synagogue hens, the *shalt nots* you burst one by one—
or was it because his *Cantos* gave you permission
to empty your battered mind into the walls of verse
that you felt a kinship and personal debt?

You called his work a graph of the American mind
so that whatever was in that mind, Dolmetsch's lute,
a fine eye gathering fire, Duccio, Rothschild, and Jewsevelt,
poured into a cracked vase bleeding syrup and lye.
Obscurities like dust blew across the page.
Raw jokes, fits of sweetness, Chinese characters, the doge of Venice,
dull history of Adams and Jefferson, ledgers and correspondence,
Yeats downstairs, a peacock *in the proide ov his oiye*—
Irish black Yiddish vaudeville routines,
exact details with small significance,
Vasco da Gama wore striped pants—
and then, rising out of the mutter and ripple of mind,
an upturned nipple, bronze in the light
—the light Pound saw and made us see—
so that you, Allen Ginsberg, the biggest Jew in po bizness,
would hunt him down in Venice to plant a kiss on his cheek.

He was by then a broken man besieged.
"We get hippies," his Olga said.
One pitched a tent in the garden, she ran him off with a hose.
Journalists rang the bell "announcing they will tell both sides.
What do they think we are? Ezra Pound is no pancake."

You came in the summer of '67,
chanting *Hare Krishna* outside his window,
back from India, Morocco, Japan,
another stop on your wisdom journey:
Martin Buber, Jerusalem's sage,
and your first Tibetan teacher, Dudjom Rinpoche.
Eyeing your hippie entourage, Olga asked,
"Would you like to wash your hands?"
But you said, "Do you people need any money?"
Olga thought you "a big lovable dog
who gives you a great slovenly kiss
and gets lots of hair all over you."

Dog Jew, hairy Jew—Allen, who sent you?
Did you stop first in Rome for Primo Levi's blessing,
whose hands trembled in Birkenau?
Did you sing *Hare Krishna* outside Paul Celan's window
before he jumped into the Seine
or say kaddish for his mother, murdered by men
who also had theories about economics and race?
Was there a depth of kindness in your public relations?
Were you able to hold not only forgiveness
but the knowledge of all that needed forgiving?

You met again that fall, at the Cici restaurant in Venice.
You in dark glasses, rich Adamic beard.

Pound's thin aged face, wisps of white hair.
Across the table you asked to say
"more than a few words."

You did most of the talking, Pound in his silence and regret.
Then pausing in the yakety-yak of your eternal sentences,
you asked, "Am I making sense?"
To which Pound said, "Yes," and then mumbled,
"but my poems don't make sense.
Any good I've done has been spoiled by bad intentions."

Then very slowly, with emphasis,
"But the worst mistake I made was
that *stupid suburban* prejudice
of anti-Semitism."

So Pound half confessed to a bearded Jew,
for a Jew he saw in you, not a Buddhist,
with the Jewish fire and sweetness and the eagerness to explain.

From the time you heard Blake's voice in Harlem
you butted your head against the Hebrew God
until Buddha lifted your prophet's mantle
when Rinpoche told you,
"If you see something horrible, don't cling to it.
If you see something beautiful, don't cling to it."

You told Pound, "I come to you as a Buddhist Jew."
Fair enough. He shouldn't think himself
forgiven by the other kind.

Or was it Martin Buber who sent you
when he told you to forget
the voices of angels and demons,
"Our business is with the human."

Pound learned that in the iron cage,
you in the asylum.
Celan knew it, but couldn't live with it.
Primo Levi knew it, but let go of the rope.

Whoever sent you, Jew or Tibetan,
when Ezra confessed you forgave.
"Do you accept my blessing?" you said.
Pound, "I do."

But a year later, outside a McDonald's
(in our strange American life),
Pound shuffled off into the woods.
Laughlin found him muttering,
"Why don't you just discard me here?"

Now in the suburbs of Elysium,
Ezra Pound, wander as you will
past Big Mac wrappers and a few extra fries.
Go into the dark woods where Dante roamed
and hear once again the clear sweet voices
that drove you to make a beautiful thing.

Or crack your pot against the stone of time.

And you, Allen Ginsberg, in the land of 10,000 Buddhas,
or in the simple heaven of your mothers and fathers,

or raw bone under the earth,

                    tell me, which is it now?

"If you see something beautiful, don't cling to it"?
Or is our business with the human after all?

My Holocaust

Don't remember talking about it much as a child.

Faces of men in striped pajamas
behind barbed wire, blinking at the light.
Their flesh soapy, unnatural. Their time
on earth slowed down to forever,
their waiting a new unit of time.

My eyes, their eyes. My flesh, their flesh.
My bones, their bones. My Holocaust
is a museum, a movie, a TV show.
A few old folks with tattoos who can say,
I was there, and soon enough
they will step out of the light.

My Holocaust is a book of fine print.
The names of dead relatives
I never knew recited in a small synagogue,
a chamber of memory where the *khaz'n*
is fat and seedy in the shadows.

In a museum in Washington a tourist
holding an ID card shuffles past cases
though no ID card will link me
to bits of crunched bone, crushed into flesh.

What can I take home as a souvenir?
Pity is too cheap and the history
of the Jews is not their deaths.

And I have no idea, dear Khaz'n,
how to join you in your reedy prayer and chant,
a saxophone of spittle in your throat,
how to lift the obscure Aramaic of mourning
through seven heavens of praise
dragging the roll call of the dead
behind us like boxcars
through a Poland of smoke.

My Holocaust is a dozen wooden synagogues,
dollhouses on a table, for hundreds burned—
all of them, in Russia and the Ukraine.
The list of slaughtered towns
covers a wall that can't be read,
thick and obscure as dried blood.

My Holocaust is Europe without her Jews.
A pleasant Europe of shops,
prosperous boulevards,
fine art, and no Jews.

Judenstrassen where there are no *Juden,*
Jewless Jew towns, and in small shtetls,
the broken walls of a synagogue
pen pigs while an old man
who witnessed the slaughter
tends a cemetery of weeds.

Will my people reduced to a loud fraction
join their old friends the Hittites,
Jebusites, Moabites?
Lost tribes, lost languages, ruined temples,
gods and goddesses suspended
in a Lucite case.

When a people disappears, they leave
opaque, inexplicable names.
Ouachita.
Tallahassee. Mississippi.

Death is a solvent breaking the bonds
of word and object, fist and song,
marching orders and boots
that crushed small hands, the whips and dogs
whose teeth sank into particular flesh
and routed from an attic a trembling boy
whose name is lost. The cry of a child
and then the night was still
and the full moon continued its passage,
a great white boat carrying nothing.

The smoke left the chimneys rising
according to physical laws, and bodies in motion
remain in motion, and bodies at rest
disintegrate, their names break down
into letters and hollow breaths
of lost vowels. And bodies burned remain
ashes buried or scattered. So why should
memory be more permanent,
more sacred, than our flesh?

In my Holocaust Theme Park you will see
a river of blood, a mountain of gold crowns.
Here in the Fun House
it's a scary ride down into the tunnel
of broken teeth and children's shoes.

And what do I teach my children?
To be angry, not to be angry,
to hate the haters, to love them,
to love everyone, to hate everyone,
to remember, to be a little afraid,
to learn how to forget,
to be a Jew out of pure revenge,
to teach Hitler a lesson?
Who should I forgive and who
is now to be forgiven?
Naked bodies in piles that
cannot be untangled or unremembered.
The sparks in our souls are tired of leaping,
tired of bearing all these names
in Hebrew, Yiddish, Polish, and pure will.

When you leave the Fun House
you will get a blue tattoo,
souvenir of all lost memory,
to burn a day or two on your arm
and whatever you feel will be adequate,
for you bought your ticket for mercy
and had it stamped in sympathy,
though I wouldn't invest too many tears.
The Holocaust doesn't have a future.
Another fifty years and it's history.

Death is a great equalizer
and it is up to us to live against that fact
for the men in stripes have given me
their Holocaust to keep
and I don't know yet what to do with it.
The bodies with arms stamped with numbers
will be numbers again
unless an angel *khaz'n* with a giant mouth of prayer
chants each of their names, slowly one by one.
Or we will mourn with popcorn in a theater.

And someone is saying, "How many tickets were sold?"
And someone is asking, "Were there really six million?"
And someone is saying, "Are there really enough prayers?"

1990–2001

PART TWO

Torah

Genesis 1:1

When Gods were beginning to make
the alphabet of heaven and earth,
the wind ruffled the black waters
and the earth had no name or form.

We make impossible requests
of fundamental texts
searching in a vowel
that dissolves as we penetrate.

No name to pronounce,
no form to see and the letters
from aleph to tough
ruffle like particles of ocean.

We hover over waters
created before the beginning,
waters that spit up letters
black as ink or thought.

Adam, Earthling

I lay in a heap, a crumpled Adam,
an earthling fallen into pants and shirt,
suit and shave. My body cramped a throat
hole to breathe holy words, wrapped a vein
tight to the collarbone.
My necktie hid my voice, flesh apple
tuned to name each animal way.

Anger is the tiger, pride the lion,
lust stampedes in elephant must.
But I woke in a painful body,
tightened and punished, my bruises
were lecterns, I had no mate.
My trouble was a sky,
a darkening page of promises
made and broken.

God is not a poem but a long disaster.
The letters baked in a half-light eaten in a prison.
One by one the honeyed letters go down.
You can't eat Torah. Can't eat the story
of whale eating Jonah, of Samson licking
honey, of manna doubled on day six.
Spies return hauling grapes. The bunches
chewed stain teeth and cheeks, spill luscious
on lip and jaw. But you can't lick the page.

Letters swim into holes in the eyes,
the ear channels. Vowels wind the lungs.
Thrill pumps vessels of the heart.
You can't eat the grapes off the page, can't
eat the apple that tells the story of how
you have fallen into this world, ruined
by the apple of your eye.

The sky's bent aluminum, cloud shaft and channel.
New moon eye poked out. A cross bird wakes
and howls. New moon gospel, dawn
jump and shout, twist and sing. Notes rip flesh
like hacksaws. Fly fly fly away.

I gave birth to three seeds: indolence, arrogance,
and a third to be named. Out of the last seed:
dawn, birds, sky, moon, held in a compact dot.
I carried three seeds in my pocket.
Three letters. Three words.
Armies clashed in my wrists.
The sky predicted every war,
a history written and closed.
I knew better, a man of clay, a humus man.
I ate what I planted.
Burial taught me nothing. Death, another
click of the wheel. The lock opened—
it was always open
—and I flew like a starling out of the earth.

Adam, Golem

This is the book of the generations of Adam.
—Genesis 5:1

Your eyes saw my golem; and in your book
all things were written.
—Psalms 139:16

The panels of memory slid into their boxes.
The pages all packed away.
The page that read "me" no longer read.
The page that read "You" carefully burned.

The sky's amber suicide, and the dawn's
lettuce leaf—these were filed.
Other days were shuffled together.
The spine stamped DREAMS.
The scent of olives and tobacco.

These are the generations of Adam:
more wolfish faces, canine incisors.
Some married their sisters.
Murdered their children.
Or their children murdered them.

This is the book of Adam, thin volume.
A list of names and numbers.
Only one command. Multiply.

Now we have rules no one understands.
The index alone fills volumes,
and space cries out like an empty lot.

Be careful packing the head—
mud and dream,
likely to give off shocks.
A few fresh petals will cover the eyes.
Lock the nostrils with clay.

Noah's Grapes

Shem and Japheth . . . went backward, and covered the
nakedness of their father; and their faces were backward,
and they saw not their father's nakedness.
—Genesis 9:23

Blue, blue-green, purple. The old drunk
collapsed on the lawn is somebody's father.
The grapes hang in bunches, sweet globes
fat with seeds. They clutch the trellis.
The sun has made them thirsty, and the old man
sleeps in deep water. A film of dreams
slips across his sight, dreams of salt
and generation. His T-shirt hiked over
his swollen belly, chin grizzled, his fly
yawns. Don't wake him. Don't in any way
disturb his old dream. Or he will curse
with the curse of looking backward,
drowning in a sea forty years deep.
The rainbow is old and put away. The rain
that fed the grapes until they burst,
until the raven and dove gorged themselves,
has dried up in the gnarled roots. Call the cops
if you want, but don't wake him. Don't let him
see you seeing him. It's not worth looking at.
It's wizened, wrinkled, shriveled, the power used up,
the grape skin without the grape.

Naming the Angel

I have wrestled with the angel of failure.
Was he sent by my brother from across the river?
I say, "Tell me your name."

Maybe nothing moves down
the ladder but what we ask for, if in greed,
then greed, if in anger, then horned anger
gores our nights. Nothing walks down the ladder
but what we dream on the hard rock.

Whether the stars will come out tonight or cold stones
from cold sockets depends on where I lay my head.
"Tell me your name." *I can't tell you.*
I have a new name each time I am sent.
My name is your desire meeting me. You have sent
your family ahead of you, and your tribe of goats and camels,
to meet me alone. My name is Alone and you have stopped
all night to defeat me Alone. But your brother
waits for you on the other side of Jabbock.
Lonely, you have made yourself Alone.

The Broken Tablets

R. Joseph learnt: . . . both the tablets and the fragments
of the tablets were deposited in the ark.
—BT Menachot 99a

The broken tablets were also carried in an ark.
Insofar as they represented everything shattered,
everything lost, they were the law of broken things,
the leaf torn from the stem in a storm, a cheek touched
in fondness once but now the name forgotten.
How they must have rumbled, clattered, on the way
even carried so carefully through the waste land,
how they must have rattled around until the pieces
broke into pieces, the edges softened,
crumbling, dust collected at the bottom of the ark,
ghosts of old letters, old laws. Insofar
as a law broken is still remembered,
these laws were obeyed. And insofar as memory
preserves the pattern of broken things,
these bits of stone were preserved
through many journeys and ruined days
even, they say, into the promised land.

Reading *Gabriel's Palace*

Forests. Sleeping on a cold bed of leaves.
Ticking of grubs in the mulch. The inner ear,
intimate with balance, whorls like a thumbprint,
like a whirlwind. The dream, thick as syrup,
oozes into the wound. Deep—always deep
in the forest—always forest—the cabin no one knew.
The wise man, the weird troll, the angelic woman,
beckoned, threatened, dropped your name down a well
of voices, vanished into a pile of glowworms,
her nightgown's electric silk.
Dazed, you stumbled into the center of the story,
spoke your lines like a proverb,
took your place in the order that penetrates order,
that wheels through the circuits of moon, earth, and sun,
the great wheel of the Milky Way, locked and turning
with perfect force all the great weight of song.

Proverbs

One of a kind is too close to zero.

The soup burned the tongue, not the eye.

A friend is the enemy you dream of.

Let the heart sink so it can come up for air.

Impatience is cruelty in miniature.

Open a door before you open your mouth.

An unremembered dream is an unopened gift.

What you hate becomes a human being in the world.

Pray with words that are strange.

Loosen your nets and catch more fish.

Light a candle for each side of your heart.

Don't obey what you can't remember.

When you say what you mean, you add oxygen to the room.

Fame is a sarcophagus.

The you is softer than water, the I is harder than diamond.

Art is a temporary solution to a permanent problem.

Our opinions protect us from our experience.

Forgive yourself before anyone else has to.

Be patient with impatience.

The mind is a moment late to the movie of the world.

If you never lose your balance, you can't dance.

First share songs, then share secrets.

Now is as much bud as flower.

Every ten seconds is the day of repentance.

Amnesia and guilt are estranged sisters.

Hope burns the hopeless.

The eye lights up from within.

It was dark, so he closed his eyes.

In a sea of light, he is looking for a firefly.

Kindness is transparent.

Time is another name for God.

In all my agony, I heard a familiar sound.

Solitude is the way silence becomes the whisper of the first word.

Dogs bark most at other dogs.

Altneuschul, Prague, Tisha B'Av

This house sunk below the street
—some say "from envy," some
"from fear of flood"—is dim
tonight, a Gothic ship
with solitary mourners
floating in the hold,
our wooden prayer stands overturned
as if by wrenching storm.

Enclosed in hewn stone, a twin nave,
our little ship, our vault.
The *khaz'n,* grumpy mate,
distrusts the stranger, is slow
to hand me a book. He thinks
I'm just an odd deckhand, a drifter
who can't put his strength to oar
and turn the song against the wave
of centuries. I hunch over
Lamentations'
tiny print pressed together,
each Hebrew letter like a wheel
of spikes or stings, each word a row
of gears, turning to the ancient chant
which I inhale
—then spin the wheels
myself, moving them with song.

Oy and oy and *Eicha* which is *ache*
though it means how.
"*How* does the city sit solitary
that was full of people—*Eicha*.
How is she become a widow
who was great among the nations?"

Some rest on wood, some sit on stone.
Our mourning is a diamond
of all the nights that crushed us,
its points hard and bitter,
yet brilliant to the tongue.

This night we visit every year
the scene of desolation.
"He has set me in dark places
as those who are long ago dead.
He has made my chain heavy.
Even where I cry and call for help
He stops up my prayer.
He has enclosed my ways with hewn stone.
He has made my paths crooked."

In tinier print, these words
are repeated out of mercy:
"Turn us to You,
O Master of every wave,
turn us to You
and we will be turned."

PART THREE

In the House of Mourning

13

Two feet, ten fingers, one head.
Or I will build you 13
out of the teeth in her jaw, the bone
in her skull, the orbits, the sockets,
soapy calcium, brash dentine.
13 the unlucky, 13 the tattoo
on the breast of the convict.
Out of 13 I can build you
ten attributes of God, then 3 beyond beyond.
I can take you from world to world
on a ladder or give you just this:
yod, gimel. Fingertip camel.
13 the irreconcilable, how we hate in our hearts.
13 the friction, 13 the glamour,
13 that shines but we are afraid to touch.
Two pupils, two earholes, two nostrils, one mouth,
four chambers of the heart, two puffy lung bags.
The sound bursting through the holes, the sacs, the ventricles,
or in the rigor mortis of anger.
Suicide 13, oddball 13, unlucky 13.

Sparrow Land

Three tiny dreams, then nothing.
Not her voice with all its lead and gold.
Not her hand which held the aluminum spatula under the burnt liver.
Not her eyes which housed me and light.

My head on the pillow, nothing.
Gray fog and lights, folds of raw carpet.
She had no more dreams to give me.
She gave them away in the bus terminal
where one city leads to another.
She gave them to travelers.

I learned her like rhymes.
Her eyes were ice.
Her hands are sand.
Her fists were rocks.
Her tongue stung.

Can anyone say what the words are
what the words are that will heal
that will heal, concealing a dove
cupped in the palm of her hand?

Messenger pigeon.

Heads Will Roll

> If you wait by the river long enough,
> you'll see your enemy's head float by.
> —Proverb

Hillel, rabbinic sage, once saw
a skull float by on the river.
"Because you drowned others,
they have drowned you.
Because they drowned you,
they shall drown too."

Sarmad, Sufi poet and saint,
when the executioner came near,
greeted him with "O my beloved . . ."
His head rolled down the steps
and would not stop singing.

Standing on the dream bridge half awake
with night in its terrible robes
of moonlight and black cloud,
I see a head floating by.
Why, with a smile on its face?
What song does the river sing?

Morning Prayers in the House of Mourning

I was leading the prayers in the living room
calling out your name, your name in disguise,
its hundreds of faces, its old Aramaic,
its Hebrew and psalm, its wished-for decrees,
its forgiveness for life, the dead unnamed.
The old chant with its twisted bit of damage,
lilt and singsong, seesaw cry, up and down
to the suburbs of heaven, step, stumbling step.

And all that time you were in the next room
with my father's face, at a computer screen.
You said to me, "Why are you singing 'Elohai N'shama'?"
And I answered "Because *My God, the soul is pure . . .*"
I said that to you! I thought I was the injured party.
You said nothing more while the modem
screeched its raw cries of connection.

Uncle Louis, or Why My Father Moved
from Baltimore to Florida

Just now my cherry-tomato plant, December late afternoon,
holds three hard green balls on prongs—a pawnshop sign—
this late in the year, not enough sun to ripen them.

Who pawns what, as the zebra caterpillar crawls on the butterfly
    weed to gnaw
a last sweet leaf, leaving the stalk bare as a phone pole on a cold
    backstreet
in Newark, twenty years gone.
There my uncle Louis, the cheap landlord, tore their porches off
when the Puerto Ricans complained they were rotten,
and piled up his pennies and nickels into a massive heart attack
that scared my father to Florida out of Baltimore's cold winter;
that and the small black mouth of a pistol pointed to the back of his
    skull
as he lay on the drugstore floor with an eyeball on the dirty vinyl.

62 years old, and the addict scooping money and pills from his safe,
storehouse of money and controlled substances,
of thirty years pacing vinyl past the register and the pill counter,
the scale with brass weights he hardly ever used
any more than the scale of nature
that balances three green tomatoes against December's failing light,
green babies that will never ripen or grow.

But it wasn't the pistol that sent him packing.
My father's brother's death reminded my father of death
in a rich and obvious rhyme. And if it's true the sum
of any man's life is zero, that's only in simple math.
The years can balance on the tiptoe of a moment
in an elephant ballet, weighted with music and destination.

But lying on the floor of his pharmacy facing death
he thought of the police, the alarm, but did not yet think of his life.
He was strangely calm in eternity where the emergency took place.
He did not go to Yom Kippur where a big God writes your name
in the Book of Life and seals it with wax.
He did not whisper the Shema or say ultimate things.
He was so sure, even there on the floor, that he would always live
because it wouldn't be fair to die
when he had already sacrificed himself so many times.

So it was natural to find himself
down on his knees, then lying on the floor.
Natural to feel the cold metal mouth of the gun at his nape
and to see that the floor needed mopping
and to remember the combination of the safe
—the perfect trick of numbers—
the safe that held the money and the drugs.

Who lay on the floor and who held the gun
while judgment hung in the balance?
The unused scale held its sad empty pans and grimy brass weights.
When he got off the floor and dusted off his pants,
the alarm started ringing in his head.
After his brother Louis died later that month,
he knew it was time for a getaway.
He heard one golden word, *Florida.*

And how about the son who mocks? Who holds the gun,
who lies on the floor, who scoops the powder,
who makes the getaway, who is also the cheap brother
of the coldwater flat, tearing off the porches,
and who is the baby screaming in Spanish
when the green paint fell from the demolition
in a drizzle of lead and crept into the baby's nostrils
and stole the baby's brain. Have I done better,
unripe tomato on a prong, too late for the season?

God sits in heaven writing all these names in a golden book.
God is very careful with the spelling, with the writing down,
and the sealing wax. God writes a short message
after each name. I am tiptoeing up to the table
with the golden book and the brass scale,
hoping to sneak a peek. Hoping I'm included.
As if God doesn't see me.
As if God doesn't watch the cold green tomato.
As if the scales aren't being used every moment.
As if God wasn't there with my father on the floor.
As if God doesn't know where I stand in the light.

PART FOUR

Blessings after the Meal

Rye

Inside a caraway seed, half forgotten,
a hint of pepper and peppermint
locked in a small black boat.
In a framework of pores—breaths
of yeast—the boats slip in
to their holes. The slightly sour
flavor of good Jewish rye—I'm
talking about the white stuff not the black—
also promises sweetness. This contradiction
is how flavor defies logic, how
in the end logic is a silly thing
even though it builds bridges and murders
millions, logic forgets the taste of rye
and wouldn't consider the crust of rye
in all its attributes: firmness, brownness,
circumference, and wisdom,
for there is wisdom in a crust that holds
the whole within its ellipse,
that restrains the moister whiteness
like the mud shore of a lake in the sun.
Again the seeds are boats. Some genius
thought of them. Probably they have
healing powers, even lodged for days
between the teeth, hitchhikers from an old
sandwich, remembrance of things pastrami.

The Color of Time

When I arrive six sharp, I cut my finger.
Six on the dot and the dot dissolves
on my lip, a tiny time capsule.
I was born in the suburbs of hurry,
she in the projects. The more that has been taken
from you, the more you need back. Time and desire.

I watched her fork stab each pea.
There isn't time in the universe
for her to finish her salad.
Yet if an angel stands beside each blade
of grass, singing "Grow, grow, grow,"
can't there be an angel to guide her fork?
An angel at her hand? An angel in her eyes?
I slept, I woke. The pile of puckered peas
the chicken she patted with her paper napkin
shrank a little. The restaurant was renovated
and her fork attacked a wisp of mashed potato
with all deliberate speed. I died several times
between sips of coffee, watched children
grow old, while the cashier rang up
money like a song and laughed and cried.
"Would you like another cup of coffee?" I asked.
(I was feeling immortal already.) What was
another universe or two compared with what
I'd spent so far—maybe a cherry pie?

Tours of Heaven

The wish-fulfilling tree repeated in a mirror.
Lotus-blossom spaceships pierce incense-trailing clouds.
Sweet weather in the land of 10,000 Buddhas.
Next door, in Mormon heaven, relatives in blue choir robes,
long lost and best forgotten, greet you at the gates.
There's lots of singing to do and nowhere to hide
in an infinite family reunion.
But just to the east is a bad boy's nightclub.
Cigarettes and party girls, booze and stag films.
The houris in transparent veils
serve scotch and kif all night.
In Jewish heaven trials all day long. Court in session:
the accused and the innocent defamed by angels.
Sins weighed with lead, good deeds with feathers,
but a good argument is so appreciated, it always
averts an evil decree. Justice rules
the realms of justice, and mercy floods the banks.
Time bubbles. We ride in an envelope of flesh,
stamped with the wrong address. It carries us
from one realm to another. Sometimes in the fist of justice,
sometimes on the waters of mercy. Reborn in lower realms
but in a stronger body, I taste again the berry globes,
black worlds, red worlds, staining my teeth.
Small criminals have sharp teeth. Nothing shall stop me
from tasting all over every delicious crime.

Turtle Soup at Mandina's

New Orleans

Gobs of meat knobbed with fat sink below my spoon.
The waiter sweeps a fifth of sherry past my nose.
The surface doused, "And more?" he asks, one eye on the next
table, crumpled bills, dead crabs sprawled on plates.
I want more, and more, the sherry clears a window
on the grease like ice on a filthy pond.
I was so hungry when I read the words *Turtle Soup*.

I swirl the sherry, it melts like salve in a wound.
A world swirls below my spoon, and a muddy river
winds through the broth, past the old Confederate statuary
and the telescope bright with Jupiter by the Café du Monde,
past the hooker in a leopard-skin bikini with a tiger tattoo,
past Port of Call and Charmaine Neville clearing notes
in the smoky air, past bottles smashed on Charity,
past Jude Acers, the chess king of Decatur, in his red beret,
past the Jackson Square shoeshine, past I-10 out of here
past a green shack in the marsh with a waterfront porch,
past the turtles lazy as rocks who sun their black shells
and drop in the muck if you as much as breathe
only to float up out of the murk in bits and pieces
at the bottom of my spoon. O generous broth, disgust
is the birthplace of taste, delicious New Orleans turtle soup.

For Borscht

A bowl of borscht. Sea of blood,
fingers of beet. Rich lump of white cream,
a sour galaxy—and stars spread
their tendrils of luminous breath.

Lights in heaven and borscht in a bowl.
Cold grandfather soup from the fridge
with a soft potato of maybe
spelunking in the depths,

old potato eye lurking in sweet red soup.
Down comes the silver spoon to divide
the mind, down comes thought and
impotent anger, immodestly, rage and outrage.

Tears dilute the soup. Laughter shakes
the bowl, the queen of knowing and acting
who holds all in her wide and generous
embrace. More borscht, please. More cold borscht.

This has to be about how one can feel
about any food, how sweet and sour mix,
and red and white. The red is from
the mother and the white is from the father,

the potato is first cousin to the beet
like grave mates side by side.
We cook the potato
in its jacket and drop it hot in the soup,

but the sour cream floats down cold
and spreads its luxury slowly.
This has to be about nourishment
and desire, or about the ground and sky.

The sky in the Ukraine must have been
like this, clear blood from the heart
of beet dug from the stubborn ground.
We ate like they ate. We died

at their hands, the borscht spilling
out of our skulls, or a rivulet
from the corner of Grandfather's mouth,
dribbling down his dark cotton beard.

I bring her home still fresh and shining
in a supermarket jar
and pour her sloppily, scattering
drops of blood on the white tablecloth,

borscht *Shekhinah,* borscht mother of us all.

You Don't Have to Be Jewish

You don't have to be Jewish to love Levy's . . . rye.

You could be black, Italian, a Cherokee
with very large teeth, grinning over a
corned beef sandwich. You don't have
to be Jewish to love, certainly or
uncertainly, you don't have to be Jewish
to love Levy's rye. Or to love anything:
a single caraway seed, or the rough black seed
of the four o'clock enclosed in pastel petals,
late afternoon. You know it's there and
you don't have to be Jewish. You don't
have to be Jewish to walk a mile
with the sun going down rosy in the park
or to love Rosy in the park or at home
(and Rosy loves you back). You don't have
to be Jewish to chew slowly, tasting the rye
breaking down into sugar. You just have to be
willing to slow time down to a poster, a still
photograph of you in your ethnic garb
in the days when ethnicity was okay not yet
terrifying or indistinct: KISS ME I'M IRISH
and kiss me again, I'm gay Italian Chinese
and NO PARKING THIS SPACE RESERVED FOR POLISH.
You don't have to be anything, really, to love.
You don't have to be Jewish. You could be anything

amazing or distinct. You could have just once
for maybe an hour, a day, forgotten you were
different. You don't have to be Jewish, you
don't have to be, to love, to love bread. You
don't have to be wry to love Jewish—but it helps.

Psalm 1

Happy is the one who . . . does not sit with scorners.
—Psalms 1:1

Just like a tree that's standing by the water
We shall not be moved.
—Civil Rights anthem

Happy,
happy is the one who does not sit
on the crooked stool,
who stands, satisfied with
one bag of sugar, of tea,
one slice of lemon,
white china, Formica countertop,
the clock with its black hands.

Happy is the one who does not sit
on the rusty seat by the broken mirror,
but closer to the register, taking in
the aroma of fresh grease and the ketchup squeezer.

Happy is tho old man with the daily news
murmuring quietly to himself day and night.
The headlines jump up and down their fonts,
but his voice is steady and he shakes his head.
Happy is the old woman quietly studying the crosswords
and filling in the blanks with pen & capitals.

Happy is the student who studies at night
with black coffee and the sugar shaker
like a white tower in the sky.

Happy is the one who slides on life
and does not stick to the griddle.
Happy is the check, added correctly,
with the smiley face and the "Thanks!"

Happy is the name of the waitress
printed on a badge
and the customer secret in his own wallet
who pulls an extra bill and lays it on the table.

Happy is the short-order cook
who forgets time and space
with a spatula and an apron.

Happy is the world outside
balanced on the appetites
that enter through the door
with the hydraulic hinge
and exit later, full and satisfied.

Happy is the air in the room buzzing
from ear to nose to mouth, tasting,
licking, inhaled, and swallowed.

Happy is the hamburger bun
with tiny flowers of wheat
like wheels and gears turning.

Unhappy is the meat,
the slaughtered cow,
the slaughterer.

Happy is one who does not mock with the *machers,*
who lives in the apartment down the street from the diner
and dwells in solitude
that's open 24 hours a day.

Happy is the one rooted like a tree in the great life,
who draws from the porous earth
sap, leaf, juice, and fruit.

Happy the bug that eats the fruit,
the fly that lurches on the flower.
Happy the radiation flying from the petal,
invisible to the eye of man.

Happy the invisible which can't be seen,
the splash of bright color in disappearing air,
the ancient webwork of filaments
under the ground, and the mushroom heads
that pop in the spring rain.

Blessed all life unknown, the burning
filament of desire that lights the hallway,
air around the subway sign.

Happy is the dust mote blowing past the door
in the breeze that makes rails in the air.
Happy is the chaff that loved the wheat
and left it without pity or sadness,
the wheat bare in the arms of the harvester.

Happy are the wicked
singing at the top of their lungs.
Happy the neurotic in the endless technicality
of their unhappiness.
Happy the quiet man in his deep meditation
disturbed by the bass of his neighbor's speakers.
When the clear image comes to him at last,
it will gather every blunt and broken noise
at the bottom of sleep
and he will see the roots of wisdom tap
the source of life, cold and stinging fresh.

Happy is the night and the path unlit in the dark.
Happy the stumbling, the falling down.
Happy the snow on the freezing body
and the lost hat and muffler.
Happy the umbrella switched to a new owner
in the afterlife of umbrellas.
Happy matter and anti-matter
and the bit more of right than left
that makes scorners scorn scorning
and the wicked turn from wickedness.

As in the motion of particles,
the motion of the creek over the rocks,
the happy disappear into the unhappy
and the unhappy recirculate into the happy
and the leaves fall into soil
and rise again as leaves:
happy, happy, and happy.

NOTES

Grandfather Clause

In the summer of 1941, the Nazi *Einzatsgruppen,* special action units, killed more than one million people as they followed the German military through the Soviet Union.

The town of Kamenetz-Podolsk, the capital of the Ukrainian province of Podolia, was the scene of a mass murder in August 1941. According to historian Raul Hilberg, 23,600 Jews were killed by the *Einzatsgruppen* there (*The Destruction of the European Jews* [New York: Holmes and Meier, 1985], 111).

My grandfather, David Kamenetz, emigrated from Russia in 1905.

A Dead Jew's Eyes

The material in italics quotes T. S. Eliot's "The Waste Land" and "Dirge."

Eliot's poem "Dirge" was the last part of the original manuscript of "The Waste Land" but was excised at the suggestion of Ezra Pound, though at one point Pound suggested placing it at the very beginning of the book, before "April is the cruellest month." Eliot also considered "Gerontion" for the beginning of the sequence, another work with anti-Semitic content. (See T. S. Eliot, *The Waste Land: A Facsimile and Transcript of the Original Drafts, including the Annnotations of Ezra Pound* [New York: Harcourt Brace Jovanovich, 1971.])

During the period of the composition of "The Waste Land," Alfred Knopf, an American Jew, published *Poems, by T. S. Eliot* (1920) at a time when Eliot was desperate to impress his father. In the year after the publication of "The Waste Land," Otto Kahn, a Jewish banker and philanthropist, offered financial support to help Eliot leave his job at the bank.

The Lowercase Jew

The general academic approach, at least until very recently, has been to ignore the blatant anti-Semitism in Eliot's poems.

The passages in italics used in the "prosecution" are from Eliot's work. Bleistein and Sir Ferdinand Klein are Eliot's characters.

Hyam Plutzik wrote a courageous poem, "For T.S.E. Only," attacking him for his anti-Semitism.

Allen Ginsberg Forgives Ezra Pound on Behalf of the Jews

Quotations come from Humphrey Carpenter's biography of Pound, *A Serious Character* (Boston: Houghton Mifflin, 1988), and from my interview with Allen Ginsberg in May 1992, which was included in *The Jew in the Lotus: A Poet's Rediscovery of Jewish Identity in Buddhist India* (San Francisco: Harper, 1994).

Rinpoche (pronounced "RIN-po-shay," with the accent on the first syllable), or "precious one," is the Tibetan honorific for certain teachers.

My Holocaust

The poem in part is a response to two events: the opening of the United States Holocaust Memorial Museum in Washington, D.C., where visitors receive an identity card that links them to a specific victim, and Steven Spielberg's film *Schindler's List.*

The *khaz'n* is the chanter of prayer, the cantor.

"A dozen wooden synagogues" refers to the beautiful synagogues made entirely of logs that Jews built in Russia and the Ukraine. The Nazis systematically burned them all. I saw the models in a museum in Paris.

Genesis 1:1

The first line of Genesis in Hebrew is usually mistranslated as "In the beginning God created the heaven and earth." As Rashi points out, a better translation would be, "When God was beginning to create . . ." The form of the God name used in the opening of Genesis is *Elohim,* which is plural.

Taf (pronounced as "tough") is the last letter of the Hebrew alphabet.

Adam, Earthling

The Hebrew name Adam, from *adamah,* or "earth," could be translated as "earthling."

A Hebrew month begins with a new moon.

Noah's Grapes
Compare Genesis 9:19–25.

Naming the Angel
See Genesis 32:23–33.

Reading *Gabriel's Palace*
The poem is for Howard Schwartz, a poet and collector of Jewish folklore, including his volume *Gabriel's Palace: Jewish Mystical Tales* (New York: Oxford University Press, 1993).

Altneuschul, Prague, Tisha B'Av
The Altneuschul is the Old-New Synagogue of Prague. Tisha B'Av commemorates the destruction of both the First and the Second Temples in Jerusalem. It is the custom to sit on the floor and read the Book of Lamentations by candlelight. *Eicha,* literally "how," is the first word and refrain.

13
In Hebrew, *13* would be represented by the letters *yod* (10) and *gimel* (3). The shapes of these letters suggest they derive from pictographs of a fingertip and a camel.

The Color of Time
The poem is for Connie Porter.

For Borscht
In talmudic understanding, a child is formed from the blood of the mother's womb and the sperm of the father. All the white parts of the body (teeth, bones) are from the "white," and the red parts of the body (organs, blood) are from the "red" (BT Nidah 31a).

Shekhinah, literally the "dweller," refers to the Divine Presence. The Hebrew word for *temple* is *mishkan,* from the same three-letter root (*sh-kh-n*), and means "place where the divine dwells." After the destruction of the Temple, the *Shekhinah* was said to go into exile with the Jewish people.

ACKNOWLEDGMENTS

I want to thank Afaa Michael Weaver for his generous help in reading the manuscript and Richard Katrovas for his many kind and helpful readings and suggestions. Great thanks also are due to Robert Esformes and to Jon Gregg and the Vermont Studio Centers for two summers of art and spirit.

I am grateful to the following publications in which these poems appeared:

Crazyhorse: "13"

Double Dealer Redux: "Turtle Soup at Mandina's"

Exquisite Corpse: "The Lowercase Jew"

Forward: "Allen Ginsberg Forgives Ezra Pound on Behalf of the Jews"

Image: "My Holocaust"

Jewish Spectator: "Tours of Heaven" and "Noah's Grapes"

Judaism: "Genesis 1:1"

Louisiana Cultural Vistas: "The Broken Tablets" and "The Color of Time" (published as "CPT: Colored People's Time/Connie Porter's Time")

Louisiana English Journal: "The Color of Time" (published as "CPT: Colored People's Time/Connie Porter's Time")

Michigan Quarterly Review: "The Lowercase Jew"

Natural Bridge: "Adam, Earthling"

New Orleans Review: "Poem-in-Law" (published as "My Poem in Law")

Prairie Schooner: "Proverbs" (published as "Thirty Proverbs"), "Grandfather Clause," "Reading *Gabriel's Palace*" (published as "Gabriel's Palace"), and "The Broken Tablets"

Tikkun: "Naming the Angel" and "You Don't Have to Be Jewish"

"Grandfather Clause," "Gabriel's Palace," and "The Broken Tablets" in *The Prairie Schooner Anthology of Contemporary Jewish American Writing,* edited by Hilda Raz (Lincoln: University of Nebraska Press, 1998).

"Turtle Soup at Mandina's" in *Uncommonplace: An Anthology of Contemporary Louisiana Poets,* edited by Ann Brewster Dobie (Baton Rouge: Louisiana State University Press, 1998).

"Rye" and "The Broken Tablets" in *Dancing on the Edge of the World: Jewish Stories of Faith, Inspiration, and Love,* edited by Miriyam Glazer (Los Angeles: Roxbury Park/Lowell House, 2000).

"Grandfather Clause" in *Jewish American Poetry: Poems, Commentary, and Reflections,* edited by Jonathan N. Barron and Eric Murphy Selinger (Hanover and London: Brandeis University Press, 2000).

"For Borscht" in *American Diaspora: Poetry of Displacement,* edited by Virgil Suárez and Ryan G. Van Cleave (Iowa City: University of Iowa Press, 2001).

"Allen Ginsberg Forgives Ezra Pound on Behalf of the Jews" in *Best Jewish Writing 2003,* edited by Arthur Kurzweil (San Francisco: Jossey-Bass, 2003).